GOING FOR GOAL

Alan Shearer

Virgin

First published in Great Britain in 1995 by
VIRGIN PUBLISHING LTD
332 Ladbroke Grove
London
W10 5AH

A catalogue record for this book is available from the British Library.

ISBN 0 86369 907 3

Produced by **ZONE LTD**

Designed by **OFFSPRING**

Studio photography: Tim O'Sullivan/Frank Spooner Pictures
Other photography: John Peters, Action Images, Allsport, Sportsview

Printed by Proost, Belgium

CONTENTS

GOING FOR GOAL!

INTRO

Hello. Welcome to Going For Goal.

In this book I've tried to explain how I became a footballer, how I do things on the pitch and what keeps me going for goal. From being a small boy in Newcastle, when my dad first threw me a ball and kicked around with me, I've wanted to do nothing but play the game. It hasn't all been easy, and I have lost count of the number of hours I have spent working on my finishing. In fact, I still spend lots of time repeatedly striking the ball into the goal from all angles and distances.

I still practise almost every day.

I believe that scoring goals is an individual thing and there is no real fixed formula for success. But there are basic fundamentals of the game which every player should be aware of if he wants to become a prolific marksman.

In Going For Goal I have attempted to set out my methods of working and some of the inspirations which have spurred me on in my career. I hope they might help you, too.

So, enjoy the book, and remember: always keep your eye on the ball and always Go For Goal!

MY ONLY GOAL
UNDER AGE SHARP SHOOTER

If I see a football anywhere within shooting range of a set of goalposts, I can never resist the urge to hammer it home. It is the greatest feeling in the world to see the ball fly between the posts and to hear that wonderful 'swish' as it makes contact with the net. I have enjoyed the unique thrill of scoring goals for as long as I can remember.

Back in the days when I was growing up on the cobblestones of a council estate in Newcastle, the 'goals' would be a pair of garage doors, a couple of tree trunks or two jackets laid out on the grass verge.

That is where I first developed my love for striking the ball past a goalkeeper. It gave me as much pleasure in those back street games as I get today scoring goals at Ewood Park, Old Trafford or Wembley.

I was lucky to be born in a football-mad area of the north-east where you had no real choice. As soon as you could walk there would be a ball at your feet and you learned to control, dribble or kick it. I was also fortunate that I had a dad who was in love with the

Above: Here's me at five years old in our garden. I'm wearing my first Newcastle United kit.
Top right: Here I'm posing for a school photo with my sister Karen. I was six, she was eleven.
Below: Grange First School FC. That's me on the right, sitting down, with my first official team.

game. He would spend hours kicking a ball to me in the back garden. Even if he had been hard at work all day or had just returned from an afternoon out with his mates, I would tug at his sleeve and drag him out for a kick-about. He never complained.

Mum and Dad were not well off by any means but I never seemed to go without anything, whether it was the best pair of boots or shinpads on the market or the latest Newcastle United strip.

When I started school I took part in organised games and I knew there was only one thing I wanted to do in my life - become a professional footballer.

Inevitably, my schoolwork suffered. I wasn't interested in doing any of my lessons. I couldn't wait for break or lunchtime so that I could get the football out. If there was no ball available, a brick or a tin can would do. When my teachers tried to explain there was very little chance of making it as a footballer, I ignored them. There was nothing else on my mind.

Mum and Dad urged me to take more of an interest in other things but I think they

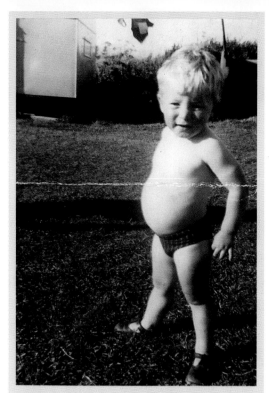

soon realised they were wasting their time.

Once, when we had to complete a careers form, I wrote, for a bit of fun, that I wanted to be a dustman. My dad gave me a clout for that and made me put down 'joiner', but both he and I knew my heart was set on playing football and nothing else.

I played for all my school teams at Grange First, Gosforth Central and Gosforth High, mostly as a striker but sometimes in midfield. I remember there was a bit of rivalry between myself and a lad called Andrew McTaggart over who would be captain of the school team and when I got the job I was walking on air.

I recall my first injury at the age of eleven. I went into a tackle and the impact of it pushed the bottom of my shinpad, where there was no foam, into my leg. It caused a deep cut which required six stitches and for a few days I was hobbling around the playground on crutches. It hurt like mad but it made me feel really grown up - almost like a real footballer.

As well as playing for my school

Above left: That's me kneeling at the front right-hand end of the team. It was at an under 13s six-a-side tournament at St James's Park. We won!
Above right: Here's me aged one at my nan's caravan in Scarborough. If I turned up for training with a belly like that I'd get hell!

teams, I also turned out for the Wallsend Boys Club, where in previous years players like Peter Beardsley and Steve Bruce developed their skills. We won just about every league and cup competition for five years and I was a regular on the score sheet.

But I can recall one match where I just could not hit the target. We were winning 13-0 and I had squandered several chances, as well as hitting the bar a few times. My dad was goading me on from the sidelines. He used to call me 'Smoky' because of my love for smoky bacon crisps and he yelled out to me, 'Bet you a pound you can't score, Smoky.'

That was a challenge I couldn't ignore, and in the next five minutes I had three touches and scored a hat-trick.

The joy of playing football was enough for me in those days but I found it a useful way to earn some extra pocket money as well. I used to play one-against-one with my mate Gary Hayes in the street near our house for 10p a goal and sometimes I would finish £1 in profit.

My first real step towards becoming a professional footballer came when I was twelve. Every club employs scouts (men who watch young lads play football) who, if they think that a lad might make it as a professional, tell the club to give him a trial, sign him up or maybe just keep an eye on him.

I was discovered by Jack Hixon, a lovely man who even today is a close friend. Jack turned up one day when I was playing for the Newcastle City schoolboys team. His 'beat' is the whole of the north-east, and any promising young player in that vast area is sure to come under Jack's gaze at some point. He must have seen something in me that he liked, because he came along for a second look when I was in action for Wallsend Boys Club.

Pretty soon afterwards Jack asked my dad if I would like to go and have a trial with Southampton. My dad replied, 'Ask him yourself, he's old enough to make up his own mind.' That was typical of Dad. He wanted me to be responsible for my own actions, and didn't want to put any pressure on me.

Of course, I was still a Newcastle United nut in those days, and had recently been there for a trial. In later years a myth would develop about my trials for The Toon - that Newcastle did not see me playing as a striker because I spent the whole of the trial playing in goal. But that was not really the case. I did take a turn between the posts, but so did everyone else on trial that week. I spent a

This is me aged sixteen, having just signed for Southampton as a YTS trainee. You can see how happy I am! All I ever wanted to do was play football, and I've been lucky to do it.

fair while playing outfield as well.

I jumped at the offer to go for trials at Southampton because I felt it would give me the chance to compare different clubs.

Five of us travelled from the north-east to Southampton during the school holidays. Everyone stayed in a big dormitory just outside the town. I soon realised how much competition I faced. The top schoolboy players from all over the country attended the sessions.

THE FIRST BREAK

After three appearances as a sub for The Saints, I played my first full game at The Dell, against Arsenal. I had a dream start to my career when I scored a hat-trick. I was only seventeen, and still hold the records for being the youngest player to score three goals on his debut, and the youngest player to score a hat-trick in the First Division.

I was on the verge of being booted out at one stage, but I managed to score a goal in a game which persuaded Southampton to give me another chance. Eventually I was taken on as a trainee and I was on cloud nine. I had taken my first big step towards achieving the only ambition I ever had. They presented everyone who was being taken on with a tie, and I cherished it as though it was made of gold.

Even though it meant turning my back on my beloved Newcastle, I chose to sign for Southampton because I had a feeling that it would be a better career move and that there would be more chance of breaking into the first team at an early age with The Saints.

Jack monitored my progress, just as he did with all the lads he took to The Dell, and over the years he has become part of the Shearer family. He has been a major influence on my career, and has cost me a fortune in telephone calls. Wherever I travel, at home or abroad, I always ring Jack to chat about football and ask for his advice on all manner of things. He scouts for Sunderland now with the same insight and love for the game he has always shown.

Scouts like Jack are a breed apart. Many of them devote their lives to football, and not for the financial rewards because they only get paid for their telephone bill and expenses. When Jack recommended me to Southampton, he provided them with a player who was to become worth £3.3 million, but he did not do it for any personal financial reward. He did it for the pride of knowing he had helped a football-crazy youngster take the first steps towards realising his ambitions.

APPRENTICE SAINT
THE EARLY YEARS

My hair has grown slightly longer since this picture but Newcastle's Darren Peacock, then of QPR, has now got hair almost halfway down his back! He's one of the tough central defenders in the Premiership, of which there are a lot these days. They all have their tricks for trying to stop me – I hope they don't know all of mine for getting past them. It seemed to work this time, at least.

I joined Southampton as a fifteen year old straight from school. I moved from home in Newcastle all the way down to the south coast and at first it was not easy. I felt homesick and missed my family. It was a completely new way of life

But it turned into a great adventure which I wouldn't have missed for the world. I lived in digs, which for me was a bit like living with distant cousins I'd never met before. I was really lucky in that Maureen and Nigel Wareham welcomed me into their home. They

are both lovely people who treated me as if I was their adopted son.

I was also fortunate to have Neil Maddison at Southampton with me. He was a fellow Geordie who joined the club on the same day as me and we forged a friendship which is as strong today as it ever was. In fact, he was best man at my wedding!

Being at Southampton helped me to grow up quickly and make my own way in the world, which was one of the reasons why I chose to join The Saints in the first place. I was paid £25 a

week and given £40 a month for a bus pass. Because Neil Maddison and I lived just five minutes away from the ground, we used to pocket our travel allowance and use it as extra spending money.

Southampton's ground, The Dell, will always be special for me. It is where I was taught my trade as a footballer back in the days when it was by no means a glamorous way of life. I had to work hard and play hard, and learn all about discipline and obedience. All of the trainees had to carry out routine chores - like cleaning boots, sweeping out the dressing room, disinfecting the medical room and carrying out any other odd jobs which needed doing.

The then-Saints full back Mark Dennis was on my list of players whose boots I had to clean. He had a bit of a reputation as a wild man, but I always got on great with him. At Christmas it was traditional for the professional players to give us trainees a cash hand-out. Mark offered me a gamble instead. He put £1 and £50 under two cups and asked me to choose one or the other. The thought of picking up two weeks' wages as a bonus was too great for me to ignore. Of course, I picked the cup with only £1 under it. But Mark was generous to a fault, and he gave me £20 anyway.

Most of the time we apprentices would work hard trying to perfect our

Above: I demonstrate, in a First Division game, how to control the ball with my chest, as someone's flying boot comes in behind me.

Above: Looking good in Southampton's 1988/89 second strip!

Below: Waiting for a corner, breathing deep. Someone is paying close attention to where I'm standing — note the pointing finger.

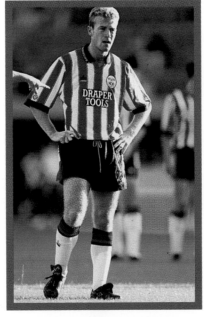

skills every day. Any spare time was spent visiting each other's digs, playing snooker or going to the cinema.

The youth team coach, Dave Merrington, was my favourite boss at Southampton. He was another fellow Geordie and we always got on well. Not that it earned me any special favours. Once, when I was arguing that it was not my turn to do a particular job, Dave overheard me and said, 'I'll show you whose turn it is, bonny lad. Be at the ground at seven o'clock in the morning, ready to start work.' On another occasion, I left a tap running in the bootroom where I had to scrape the mud off the senior players' boots and clean them. It flooded the medical room below. That made me very unpopular with the other apprentices because we were all made to run 50 laps around the pitch. Dave's argument was that it is a team game and we should share our punishment as well as our praise!

I knew that by joining a relatively small club like Southampton the chances of me breaking into first-team football would be much higher than if I joined one of the bigger clubs. I had to show I was good enough, of course, but the opportunity came to me when I was only seventeen, and I was determined not to let it slip away.

Southampton is full of fond memories for me, and I shall probably settle there again when I finish my playing career.

GOAL-DEN TOUCH
GOALD STRIKE!

I was just seventeen and still an apprentice when I was picked for the Southampton senior side for the first time - in a match against Arsenal.

My dream was about to come true. I was to step out in front of a big crowd against one of the country's glamour clubs. I was not going to mess it up. I was going to make my mark.

Even a script writer could not have come up with a better plot. I finished up scoring not once but three times on my debut. These were the first steps I had to take towards the top of my profession and although there was still a long way to go, my journey was underway.

I had scored my first goals in a league which many felt was the toughest in the world. The goals continued to flow afterwards but the very first remains at the top of this, my list of ten all-time favourite goals:

1. My first for Southampton against Arsenal. Colin Clarke crossed and I reached it ahead of the Gunners defence to score with a header which went into the net through John Lukic's legs. What a start! Unbelievably, there was more glory to follow.

2. My third in the same game. I hit the bar with my first shot from another Colin Clarke cross but managed to stab in the rebound to complete my hat-trick. I was already feeling tired, but I went off on a celebration run which just about finished me. I had to be substituted soon afterwards. After the final whistle I was presented with the match ball autographed by all the players, which I gave to my mum and dad.

3. My first goal for England on my debut against France. I was already bursting with pride after being awarded my first international cap, so you can imagine how it felt to hit the target in my opening game. It was not a spectacular effort but one I treasure. Mark Wright headed a corner down and I swivelled and beat the keeper with a shot on the turn.

4. My first for Blackburn - against Crystal Palace. I had just become Britain's most expensive player after my £3.3 million move from Southampton and while the size of the fee didn't worry me, I knew my every move would be scrutinised. I had a poor first half and sat in the Selhurst Park dressing room during the interval thinking, I'm going to get caned by the Press if I carry on like this. My chance to put things right soon came. Mike Newell headed the ball down and I beat Nigel Martyn with a volley from about 25 yards. I scored a second soon afterwards and suddenly I was being hailed as a £3.3 million superstar!

5. The opening goal of the 1991/92 season for Southampton against Tottenham. My mum had rung me before the game to tell me that Dad had put a bet on me being the first goal-scorer of the new campaign. After two minutes I collected a throw-in from Jeff Kenna and beat Eric Thorsvedt from 20 yards. My dad pocketed a few pounds and I was off the mark in style.

6. My hat-trick goal against Queen's Park Rangers in the 1994/95 season. This was one of my most spectacular efforts. I had already scored twice and we were well in command when I collected the ball 25 yards out. My team-

ALAN
"I'll never get tired of hearing that swish as the ball hits the back of the net"
SHEARER

Here's me and Graeme Le Saux celebrating my hat-trick goal against QPR in November 1994. It's always a bit special to get three in a game, as you can see from the elated look on my face!

mate Robbie Slater was screaming for the ball on my right, and to be honest he was in a much better position. In other circumstances I would have probably passed to him, but I thought I would let fly. The ball screamed into the net off the underside of the bar.

7. A crucial winner against Leeds in the 1993-94 season. We needed to win this game to keep the pressure on League leaders Manchester United. With the score at 1-1 we desperately needed to score. In such a situation tension can play some strange tricks on you. You need nerves of steel and when Graeme Le Saux provided the service, I kept calm and squeezed the ball home to give us three valuable points.

8. A precise chip shot during a 7-1 win over Norwich in the 1992/93 season. I am not normally noted for my finesse in finishing, but I was delighted with this goal. I played a one-two with Tim Sherwood and with the Norwich defence backing off me, I spotted their keeper Bryan Gunn off his line. My chip shot sailed over him into the net. The rest of the lads insisted the ball had bobbled and that I had mis-hit it, but I can assure you I meant it.

9. My first goal wearing the England colours for the Under 17 team against the Republic of Ireland at Stoke. All the people who had influenced my early career were there to support me - my mum and dad, Jack Hixon and Southampton's youth coach Dave Merrington. I stepped out proudly in an England shirt for the first time, looking my smartest, but the goal was quite a scruffy affair. A corner was flicked on and I managed to get a toe end on to the ball and force it past the keeper.

10. A header for England against the United States of America at Wembley. I was quite wound up for this game. The American defender Alexi Lalas, who had been a big hit in the 1994 World Cup finals, said before the game that he had never heard of me, and so I was unlikely to score against him. I was out to prove him wrong and when I threw myself into a diving header from a Graeme Le Saux cross, the ball flew into the net. I said to Lalas, 'I think you may have heard of me now.' It was an unnecessary thing for me to say. I should have let the goal do my talking for me, but sometimes it's easy to make regrettable remarks in the heat of the moment.

GOING FOR GOAL!
THE SEARING SHEARER TRAINING SCHEDULE

IN THE DRESSING ROOM

Match day activity starts long before the game kicks off. I try to be at the ground at least one hour before to begin my preparations. I have my own special place in the home dressing room at Ewood Park where I always sit to get ready for the match. I pay particular attention to my appearance because if you feel smart there's a good chance you will perform in a similar fashion.

Players build themselves up in different ways as kick-off approaches, and try to gee-up their team-mates. I do not have a set routine but I will often shout words of encouragement to my colleagues. As the kick-off approaches **EVERYONE IS FIRED UP AND THE DRESSING ROOM ATMOSPHERE IS ELECTRIC.**

The dressing room before a game can be tense. A lot of players like to follow a set routine for getting ready for the game. One thing I always do is strap on my shin pads. They're almost as important to me as my football boots. A mistimed tackle or collision can hurt, and do damage to my shins which might keep me out of a game or two...

STRETCHING AND WARMING UP

Once out on the pitch for the pre-match warm-up it is important to stretch as many muscles as I can. I need to be loose and supple and physically tuned up for what lies ahead. It is worth spending ten or fifteen minutes warming up the body because it can prevent serious injuries. A pulled or torn muscle could keep me on the sidelines for at least a couple of weeks and there is nothing more frustrating for a footballer than to be on the outside looking in. As the old saying goes, 'Prevention is better than cure.' All the leg muscles - groin, hamstrings, calves - need to be given a good stretch because they do most of the work in football. But I try not to neglect the shoulders, arm and neck. **THE MIND AND BODY IS NOW RIGHT - SO LET'S GO IN SEARCH OF SOME GOALS.**

Above: Stetching the thigh and hamstring muscles is extremely important. Stand with legs apart, lean your weight forward on to first one leg, and then the other. Don't lean too heavily, just slowly stretch the muscles.

Left: Bending forward along the line of a leg stretches lower and upper back muscles, as well as the hamstrings. No stretching should be done too strenuously – just feel the muscles extending and if it hurts, stop!

A footballer needs to warm up and stretch every muscle in his body. Throwing my arms back behind myself as far as feels comfortable (left) and then forward, across my chest (right) gets the circulation going in my arms, extends all my arm muscles and loosens my upper back and shoulder muscles. I hold my neck firmly forward to stretch neck muscles too.

RUNNING WITH THE BALL

The key to running with the ball is to keep it close to your feet. It is best to start with your eye on the ball but eventually you have to be aware of where team-mates are, which requires lifting the head.

When I do that, I need to have a feel for the ball at my feet, so close control and good balance is important. I have to make sure the ball becomes part of my running strides and does not slow me down too much.

Concentration is the crucial factor because if you switch off for a split second, a defender will whip it away from you.

Five Point Plan

1. Always know where the goal is
2. Try to think ten yards ahead
3. Know where the opposition are
4. Look for space to run into
5. Be aware of team-mates around you

Keep your eye on the ball; feel where it's going. Use both the inside and outside of your foot to control the pace of the ball. Make sure you have time when you lift your head to look for team-mates, and to make sure that there are no opposing players within stealing distance.

RUNNING WITHOUT THE BALL

Every player spends the biggest part of each match without the ball, so it is vital to learn the art of running off the ball, reading the game and assessing where and when the ball is going to be played to you. I always keep my head up, have a relaxed well-balanced posture and try to keep alert and ready to sprint into the best possible scoring position. Sometimes I will jog along behind the play to lose a defender, and then dart at the last possible moment into the penalty box. That makes me more difficult to mark. There are times when I have to be unselfish with my running. If I can see a colleague is moving into a good position with the ball, I will make a dummy run to take a defender away from the action, letting my team-mate in for a shooting chance.

TOP TIP
"Don't be afraid to not have the ball"
Alan Shearer

So much of my game is spent running defenders out of position, and looking for space, that I probably spend much of any game not touching the ball. This is an extremely important part of any striker's game, so I practise sprinting to put an edge on my dashes into the box. Mickey Quinn, the ex-Coventry striker who had the nickname of Sumo because of his size, used to say that he was faster than Linford Christie — over five yards. He probably was!

RUNNING DEFENDERS OUT OF POSITION

Running defenders out of position is an important skill because it enables me to open up enough space to receive a pass out of range of my marker. Hopefully that will give me the scope to turn and attack the goal. I try to stay one step ahead of the defender and keep him guessing about my next move. I always have to be aware of the offside trap and not let the defender force me to make an early run which leaves me offside. I might have to shake off my marker for a fraction of a second and take just one touch on the ball and keep a move going. **THE KEY TO RUNNING DEFENDERS OUT OF POSITION IS KNOWING WHICH OTHER PLAYERS ARE AROUND ME AND PREDICTING HOW AN ATTACK WILL DEVELOP.**

TOP TIP
"Always be aware"
Alan Shearer

Five Top Tips

1. Stay ahead of the defender
2. Stay on-side
3. Keep the defender guessing
4. Use the ball quickly
5. Know where your team-mates are

RECEIVING THE BALL WITH MY BACK TO GOAL

The best strikers in the game are those who can play just as effectively with their back to the goal and be just as dangerous as when they are in a clear scoring position. When I receive a ball I have to be aware of the position of the defender behind me. I have to be strong enough to hold off his challenge and prevent him from getting to the ball. My first touch has to give me instant control. I only have a short time to consider my options, so concentration is imperative. Should I turn and confront the defender, or lay the ball off to a team-mate? **MY OPPONENT SHOULD NEVER BE SURE OF MY INTENTION WHILE I KEEP THE BALL AWAY FROM HIM.**

When I play for England, I tend to spend a lot of time alone up front, with my back to the goal. It can be a bit lonely at times, but I don't really mind it. It's when playing in this position that I have to employ all of my shielding skills, and be able to take just one or two touches before laying the ball off to a team-mate. **I CAN THEN EITHER RUN A DEFENDER OUT OF POSITION OR RUN INTO THE BOX TO RECEIVE A PASS.**

TRAPPING THE BALL WITH FEET

Close control is an essential part of trapping the ball and I have to be able to use any part of the body to bring it down, regardless of what height it comes at me. If I take it on the chest, I must keep the ball as near to my body as possible and try to drop it at my feet. I can also use my thigh or foot to stun the ball and immediately take control of a situation with the ball in my possession. Balance and concentration are essential, as is body strength, to hold off my marker when I trap the ball. I know if I take my eye off it as the ball arrives, I risk losing control and giving away possession. That is one of the worst things you can do in the game. **DEFENDERS WORK HARD TO WIN THE BALL AND THEY WILL NOT BE TOO HAPPY IF YOU KEEP LETTING THE OTHER SIDE HAVE IT BACK.**

Five Top Tips

1. Always keep the ball close to your body
2. Use thigh or foot to kill the ball
3. Concentrate on what you want to do
4. Make sure you have good balance
5. Stand up and be strong

TOP TIP
"Keep your eye on the ball"
Alan Shearer

The defender in these pictures is being polite. He's not pushing me from behind or niggling at me. In the heat of a Premiership game however, there's a lot of physical contact. Most of it's unintentional, but there are always a few players who like to let you know that they're behind you. My mate Neil Ruddock at Liverpool talks to me during the game when we meet!

TURNING WITH THE BALL AT FEET

Every time I receive the ball, my first touch is crucial. When turning with it at my feet I need to achieve instant control. By letting the ball do most of the work, I can turn swiftly and confidently. The objective is to swivel quickly with as little fuss as possible so I can be ready to attack the goal. It should be a fluent and natural movement but again, concentration is the key word. **IT IS IMPORTANT TO BE ABLE TO COLLECT THE BALL WITH THE INSIDE AND OUTSIDE OF BOTH FEET SO THE DEFENDER IS UNSURE ABOUT WHICH WAY YOU ARE GOING TO TURN.**

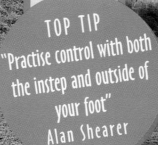

TOP TIP
"Practise control with both the instep and outside of your foot"
Alan Shearer

THE DIVING HEADER

The diving header is all about bravery. I have to put my head in low, where the boots are flying, and it sometimes results in a painful kick in the head. It is worth the risk and discomfort, though, if one diving header in ten results in a goal. I need a good spring in my legs to launch myself forward while never losing sight of the ball. I usually lead with my arms, and pull them back as I throw myself at the ball and make contact with my forehead. **I HAVE TO SWITCH OFF FROM THE POSSIBLE DANGERS AND MAKE SURE I GET THERE FIRST.**

Here you can see me beginning to curl, ready to push myself forward (above). I'm concentrating on the ball and my arms are going forward as I spring off, a bit like a diver would (left). I make contact with my forehead and the ball is directed where I want it to go (below), which is usually the goal!
Be sure that the header is the best way of getting the goal. There are times when you have to dive for it, but there are just as many times when a leg stretched out or even a knee will do the trick just as well, and there's less danger of getting kicked yourself.

TOP TIP
"Be brave, but not foolish"
Alan Shearer

Five Point Plan

1. Keep your eye on the ball
2. Get a good launch forward using your legs
3. Lead with your arms
4. Pull your arms back as the ball reaches you
5. Don't hesitate

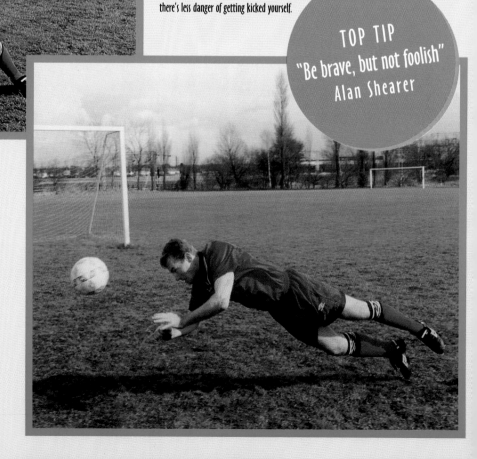

DIRECTING A HEADER AT GOAL

Here you can see me launching myself for a header from a standing start. Note that I try to keep away from the defender so as not to give away a free-kick. It's always better to get in front of the defender so you get a clear header and a better chance to get power and direction on the ball.

When the ball is crossed into the goal mouth I watch it all the way until I feel I can make contact with my head. It is better if I can have a clear run at it but sometimes I have to jump from a standing start. I raise my arms slightly to help me achieve sufficient height but I have to be careful not to make contact with my marker and concede a free kick. Good timing is essential because if I can meet the ball with my forehead as I launch myself into the air, this generates extra power. **ACCURACY IS VITAL TOO; WITH PRACTICE IT IS POSSIBLE TO TURN THE HEAD AT THE LAST MINUTE TO DIVERT THE BALL OUT OF THE GOALKEEPER'S REACH.**

TOP TIP
"Use your forehead to direct the ball"
Alan Shearer

23

DIRECTING A HEADER AS A PASS

Above: As with any header, I coil myself ready for a jump at the ball.

Below: With a defender behind me I can cushion the ball on my head and direct it to a team-mate's feet.

Strikers have a hunger to score goals but that does not mean I must try to score every time I have the ball. There are times when it is more beneficial to lay the ball off to a colleague in a better scoring position. With this in mind, it is important to be able to direct a header as a pass. The technique is similar to heading at goal, but be aware of players around you, particularly the movement of team-mates. **THE WEIGHT OF THE HEADED PASS HAS TO BE JUST RIGHT AND THIS MEANS CUSHIONING THE BALL ON THE FOREHEAD AND STEERING IT INTO THE PATH OF COLLEAGUES.**

TOP TIP
"Go for accuracy not power"
Alan Shearer

THE INSIDE, OUTSIDE, & TOP-OF-THE-FOOT PASS

When passing, I mostly use the inside of my foot to achieve maximum accuracy. It is the most natural way to kick the ball but concentration is still essential. I plant my non-kicking foot close to the ball, make sure I am balanced, keep the body over it, make a good clean contact and follow through.

If I want to be a bit more adventurous I use the outside of my foot. It is a more difficult skill but can have spectacular results. It applies swerve to the ball and can be used to deceive the goalkeeper or bend a pass round a defender. Body position has to be adjusted to allow the kicking foot space to strike the outside of the ball. A good contact is needed and if struck correctly, it will make the ball spin and swerve away in the opposite direction to that in which the ball was struck.

For shooting, I tend to use the top part of my foot. I can achieve both power and accuracy with this method. Again, position the non-kicking foot close to the ball, keeping your head still and your body well balanced. **MAKE SURE YOU FOLLOW THROUGH TO GET MAXIMUM WEIGHT BEHIND THE SHOT.**

TOP TIP
"Keep your body over the ball"
Alan Shearer

Above: Practise using all parts of your foot for control by kicking a ball against a wall, and alternately stunning it with the instep and outside. Practise kicking the ball against the wall with instep and outside and note how differently the ball travels.
Below: As ever, keep your eye on the ball when passing, but make sure you know where the ball is going, and that it's to one of your team-mates.

Above: Keeping balance is extremely important, which is why my left arm is often pointing out, away from my body. This balances my left side as my foot swings back. The arm comes in as the leg swings through.

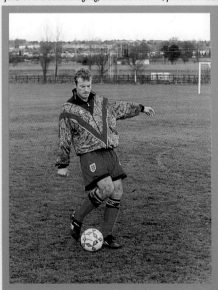

THE INSIDE, OUTSIDE, & TOP-OF-THE-FOOT PASS

Above: You can see how my left foot is alongside the ball as my kicking foot comes through. It's very important that you follow through with the kicking foot, as this helps with the power of the shot, and your own balance.

I tend to use my instep for most passes. It's simple, accurate, and can carry the right power. Again, follow through with your kicking leg.

CHIPPING THE BALL OVER THE KEEPER

TOP TIP
"Get your standing foot alongside the ball, and make sure you're well balanced"
Alan Shearer

CHIPPING THE BALL OVER THE KEEPER

Increasingly, it seems that more and more scoring chances crop up when I am through, with only the keeper to beat. I have to decide in an instant whether to try to take the ball round him or chip it over him. Keepers are a crafty lot and they can make this situation a lot more difficult than it looks. They tend to stand up for as long as possible to deny a clear view of goal. Then it becomes a real battle of wits. Attempt to make the keeper commit himself and then lift the ball over him. Keeping my eye on the ball, I plant my left foot alongside it and stab my right

TOP TIP
"Make the goalkeeper commit first"
Alan Shearer

foot underneath it. By not following through, I should lift the ball over the keeper's body and into the net. **IT IS ALWAYS WORTH FOLLOWING UP IN CASE IT REBOUNDS OFF THE POST OR CROSSBAR AND NEEDS A SIMPLE TAP IN.**

Above: Once the goalkeeper is falling one way, he gives you a clearer sight of the goal. It's easier then to put it over and past him. It can be a tense battle of nerves though.

My 100th career goal was a one-on-one with Chelsea goalkeeper Kevin Hitchcock, at home for Blackburn on Saturday 18th March 1995. Not long into the game, Mark Stein put Chelsea ahead, so we had to go flat out for an equaliser. Graeme Le Saux moved forward from left back to play in midfield, and he chipped the ball behind Chelsea defender Erland Johnsen to leave me in a one-on-one position with Kevin. Hitchcock stood upright as long as possible to deny me a good view of the target, but I simply hit it as hard as I could and the power of the shot took him by surprise.

TAKING A PENALTY

I always make up my mind which corner I am going to aim for and stick to that decision. I never change my mind because that moment of doubt can cause me to miss from the spot. Try to appear confident when you run up, keep your standing foot close to the ball and strike it firmly with the top of the foot. If I can apply pace on the ball it makes it more difficult to save, but accuracy is more important. I do not worry about the keeper's position and do not change my style because of his strengths or reputation. **I HAVE A FAVOURITE SIDE OF THE GOAL AT WHICH TO AIM BUT I PREFER TO KEEP THAT A SECRET. ONE OF THOSE CRAFTY KEEPERS COULD BE READING THIS!**

TOP TIP
"Never change your mind"
Alan Shearer

TAKING A PENALTY

Generally, if there are two or more defenders closing in on me when I receive the ball, there is no alternative but to lay it off to a team-mate. It is more difficult to turn with the ball and run at defenders when they are queueing up to tackle you. So, hold the ball up and look for someone in a better position. If I am playing as a lone striker, this will often mean waiting for a team-mate to come up in support of me. A good first touch is imperative and then you have to use body strength to keep the defenders at bay. **THE BALL SHOULD REMAIN ON THE OUTSIDE OF THE FOOT AS YOU KEEP YOUR BODY BETWEEN THE DEFENDERS AND THE BALL.**

TOP TIP
"Keep your body between th
defenders and the ball"
Alan Shearer

LONG-RANGE FREE KICKS

Accuracy is the key word when taking a free kick from outside the penalty area. If the shot is on target it has half a chance of finding the net. Every free kick is different, so I try to weigh up the options before deciding where to aim the ball. I usually go for the side of the goal blocked by the defensive wall which is furthest away from the goalkeeper. This requires a great deal of precision because you have to lift the ball over the wall and then get it to dip below the cross-bar before the keeper can get across. It might mean sacrificing a bit of power

but if the shot is on target, the keeper has a lot of ground to make up and will struggle to save it. I try to put some swerve on the ball by curling it with the inside of my foot to further deceive the keeper. **LEANING BACK SLIGHTLY AS I STRIKE THE BALL HELPS ME TO ACHIEVE SUFFICIENT LIFT ON THE SHOT AND AN ANGLED RUN UP WILL HELP TO ACHIEVE SOME BEND ON THE BALL.**

TOP TIP
"Always hit the ta
Alan Sheare

CELEBRATING A GOAL

I work all week, giving 110 per cent effort to score a goal, so when I manage to hit the back of the net during the game I feel as though all the sweat and toil has been worthwhile. Then I reckon I am allowed a moment to celebrate. I like to salute the supporters because without them there would be no professional football and then I acknowledge the part my team-mates have played in the build up to the goal. I do not go in for some of the extravagant celebrations enjoyed by some players.

TOP TIP
"Whatever else . . . enjoy the game!"
Alan Shearer

I TRY TO KEEP IT SIMPLE, BUT EVERY GOAL IS SPECIAL AND THE CELEBRATION IS MY WAY OF SHOWING HOW ELATED I AM.

ENGLAND

THE SHEARER CAP RECORD

It is always a huge thrill for me to pull on the England shirt. It's the ultimate game for any professional. I still feel very honoured when I know I've been picked to play for England, whoever the opponents are. The way Terry Venables sometimes plays the

team in his 'Christmas tree' formation leaves me alone up front, but that never bothers me. It requires a lot of hard work and running, but that is something I have always relished.

It is nice to have some company though.

It's a different game, playing in Internationals. Joe Royle, who is now manager of Everton, was a big help to me when he was in charge of the Under 21s England team and I was playing for them. As a former

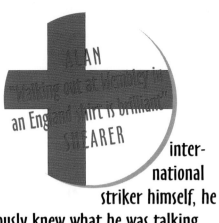

ALAN
"Walking out at Wembley in
an England shirt is brilliant"
SHEARER

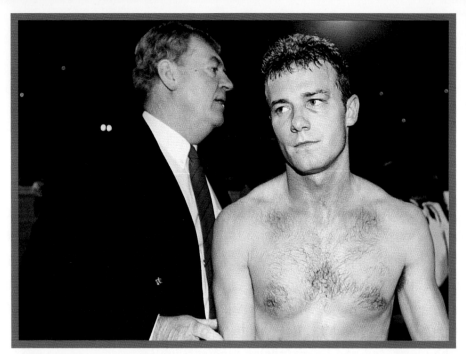

... inter-national striker himself, he obviously knew what he was talking about, and provided me with a valuable part of my football education. I scored thirteen goals in twelve games at this level and I was able to push my claims towards progressing into the senior squad. Being called up for an International at that age reminded me of my trial days at Southampton. You know you are a reasonable player in your own surroundings, but suddenly you find yourself among the best talent in your age group from around the country. The important thing to remember is that the chance to shine might not come along again, so you have to grab it when you can.

Part of the challenge of playing at international level is that you have to learn to play alongside relative strangers, and you only have two or three days to adjust to their playing styles.

I was lucky enough to make a good, early impression at every international stage. I scored on my debut for the England Under 17s against the Republic of Ireland, in my first match for the Under 21s against the same country, and on my first senior game against France.

Not that I have ever considered that I have a divine right to wear any football shirt, and certainly not an England one.

CHAMPIONS
THE BLACKBURN LINE-UP

There is always something memorable about a first - whether it is a debut for a club or country, a first goal or a first trophy. The pride of place in my display cabinet is reserved for my Premiership medal, won with Blackburn Rovers in the 1994-95 season. It was my first major honour and I remember the sweat, toil and heartstopping moments which went towards winning it in that most dramatic of climaxes to the campaign.

The Championship triumph was the perfect way to end a season which also brought me personal awards for being the Professional Footballers' Association Player of the Year and Blackburn Rovers Supporters' Player of the Year as well as the Golden Boot for being top scorer in the Premiership. The title medal was extra special because it is the big prize which every professional sets his sights on winning when he starts his career.

It is also the reward for teamwork. At Blackburn we had to take a fair bit of criticism over the course of the season from jealous people who resented the vast amount of money poured into the club by our owner Jack Walker.

There were others who disliked the way we played and claimed we used a crude direct style. When we heard such things, we closed ranks and stuck together, refusing to allow anyone to break the spirit of togetherness which saw us through the bad times.

As I wrote in my book Diary of a Season, which explains in detail the ups and downs of the title success, I considered it a privilege to be one of a collection of players who were a team in every sense of the word. This is my personal breakdown of the Rovers who became champions:

Tim Flowers

I have never seen a more complete goalkeeping performance than the one he produced in the 1-0 victory over Newcastle in our last but one game of the 94/95 season. Known as 'Cat', he loves a laugh and a joke, but few players work harder than him. If you ring him at home he will answer the phone by saying 'Safest hands in soccer' or 'England's No.1'. This is his way of taking the mickey out of himself but he believes it and so do we.

Henning Berg

He is amazingly consistent and I do not remember him having a bad game. He has shown versatility by switching from full back to centre back when

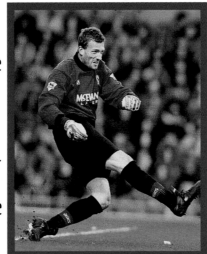

Tim Flowers likes to answer his phone with the words 'England's Number 1' or 'Safest hands in soccer'. Of course it's funny, but he likes to think it's true, and so do we. He's a great mate and a brilliant goalkeeper.

needed. I put him in the same 'Mr Dependable' category as Manchester United's Denis Irwin. Henning takes a lot of stick from the other lads because he is Norwegian but his answer is to point to his country's World Cup record in recent years and that shuts everyone up.

Jeff Kenna

He played only nine games at the end of the 94/95 season after joining us from Southampton but the club gave him a medal for the part he played in four different positions. He also scored one of the goals in an important 2-1 win over Crystal Palace, four games from the finish. He started to grow a moustache in the final few weeks of the campaign which earned him the nickname Freddie Mercury. It soon came off.

Graeme Le Saux

He has made the England left back position his own over the last couple of seasons with his performances for his club and country. No one appreciates the accuracy of his crosses from the left more than me because he has created many of my goals. He's considered a bit of an intellectual because he reads the Guardian newspaper and has an interest in antiques, but no one holds that against him.

Alan Wright

After playing for us at full back and on the left side of midfield, he joined Aston Villa in 1995 and nearly enjoyed the distinction of playing for a Championship side and relegated team in the same season. Very small and skilful, he answers to the nickname 'Dwarf'.

Tony Gale

At the start of the 94/95 season he was struggling to find himself a club. I think Barnet was his best hope until our assistant manager, Ray Harford, asked him to play in a friendly against Celtic because we were so short of players through injury. He ended up playing a significant role in the centre of our defence at the start of a season and, at 36, is the proud owner of a Championship medal. He provided us with an old experienced head when we needed it. He also gave us quite a few dodgy racing tips. He didn't get one right, but then, he didn't back them

Above: Graeme Le Saux has made the England left back position his own, and with good reason. He also moves into midfield easily. When he does, he can often be the supplier of great crosses for me.
Below: Captain Tim Sherwood is a dynamo in midfield for us and a scorer of some nice goals too.

ALAN
"All I want to do is play football and enjoy it"
SHEARER

himself!

Colin Hendry

There can be no braver footballer in the game. I can still see him when we were hanging on for victory at Everton in 1995, throwing his head and body into the thick of the action to defend our goal. Nobody is more willing to work for the club's cause than Colin and if there is a supporters' club or charity presentation going on, he will be there. He is known as the 'Blond Bombshell', although we suspect he gets his hair colour from a bottle.

Ian Pearce

He was signed from Chelsea for £200,000 when no one was quite sure whether he was a defender or a striker. He has claimed one of the central defensive positions with his strength in the air and on the ground. He is only 21 but plays as though he's 31 and you would think he'd been in the Premiership all his life. I have started to call him Eric, because I think he resembles Cantona - though only in looks.

Tim Sherwood

I have been at Blackburn for three years now and in that time Tim has just got better and better. He does all the good things expected from a midfield player - tackles, passes, scores goals and gets up and down the pitch. He fully deserved his England recognition. Tim's a cockney and a bit of a Jack the Lad character. He has an amazing head of long hair, but when I gave him stick about it, he says, 'At least I've got some - not like you.'

THE BLACKBURN LINE-UP

Mark Atkins

He filled Dave Batty's boots for most of our Championship season and did a terrific job. He weighed in with some valuable goals, most notably in the 3-2 victory over Liverpool at Ewood Park. Strong and mobile, Mark's known as 'Arrow'.

Paul Warhurst

He is incredibly versatile. Whenever there is a problem in defence, midfield, or up front, he can fill the space, though his luck with injuries has been cruel. When he joined us from Sheffield Wednesday he brought with him the nickname of 'Albert Tatlock' (an old Coronation Street character), because of his broad accent.

David Batty

With him in our team all season, the title race would probably have been over a month before it was finally decided. A foot injury restricted him to just four full appearances in 1995, and although the club wanted to give him a Championship medal, he turned it down because he didn't think he had earned one. That's typical of 'Bats'. He's a bulldog of a competitor, and has more skill than he is credited with.

Stuart Ripley

He didn't score throughout the 94/95 season, but his supply from the right wing has been invaluable, as has his non-stop workrate. In our system, the wide players are vitally important and he fits the bill perfectly. He is another intellectual who reads the Independent newspaper and does crosswords. He also has a degree in French. It's a pity

ALAN
"Kenny Dalglish is a tremendous and inspirational manager"
SHEARER

Above: Unfortunately an injury kept David Batty out of the team for most of the season, but he was an inspiration from the sidelines.
Below: Colin Hendry, the Blond Bombshell, was with us throughout the season, and played one of the best of his career.

his English is not a bit better - he's from Middlesbrough and few people can understand him!

Jason Wilcox

The biggest compliment I can give him is to say that when he was ruled out of the team for the run-in to the title, we missed him enormously. He gives us width and balance down the left and provides the sort of crosses any striker will thrive on. We call him 'The Stick' because he is so skinny, but he's deceptively strong, fast and very fit.

Kevin Gallacher

His season lasted about 67 minutes, but in that time he scored a very important goal for us against Crystal Palace before being carried off with a leg fracture. He had worked so hard to recover from a similar injury only to see his efforts go to waste, but his small contribution was very gratefully received. He's Scottish, not very big and known as 'The Moose'.

Robbie Slater

A bundle of energy who has filled in on the right and left side of midfield, and always makes his presence felt with his effort and energy. He has played in France, calls himself an Australian and played for their national team, but comes from Omskirk, just down the road from where I live. Work that out! He's called 'The Lobster' because of his red hair and face.

Chris Sutton

If you told him at the start of the 94/95 season that he would score 21 goals, he would have been delighted. He was disappointed when the goals did not flow so regularly in the second half of the season, but he still gave his all and was a major contributor to our success. He handled his £5 million move from Norwich wonderfully well, and is popular in the dressing room. He was known as 'Trigger' (because he looks like the character from Only Fools and Horses) when he joined us, but when we're feeling generous to him we call him 'Sooty'.

Mike Newell

He had an almost permanent place on the bench after recovering from a knee injury but, when called upon as substitute, he can come into the side and steady things by holding up the ball in tight situations. Another great lad to have around for team spirit, he is known as 'Mr Angry' because he has a short fuse. He would argue that black is white!

My nickname?

I was known as 'Shocks' in my Southampton days, and I haven't got a clue why. Since my move to Blackburn a few people have started calling me 'Billy Big Pockets'; a nickname given to me by our groundsman at Ewood Park, Steve Patrick, after he read in a newspaper how much I was supposed to be earning each week.

More seriously though, it was a real thrill to play a part in a Championship side and score 34 League goals, equalling Andy Cole's record set the previous season. But in addition to my goals total, I am also immensely proud of the fact that I was the only member

Above: Chris Sutton had a hard job coming to the club for so much money, but his goals soon silenced the critics.
Below: The Premiership trophy is the first major trophy of my career. It means a lot, being the first, but hopefully there'll be a lot more to come with Blackburn Rovers.

ALAN

"Goals are important to me. I've always got the number I've scored at the back of my mind"
SHEARER

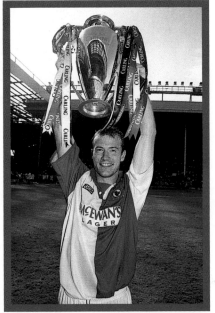

of the squad to play in all 42 League games. I remember how, at the start of the 94/95 season, people were wondering whether I would be the same player after rumours that I was suffering a serious illness.

There were times when I played with an injury, others when I turned out after a pain-killing injection, but it was never an ordeal to figure in the most exciting Championship race for years. Remember, the 94/95 season was only Blackburn's third in the top division, and never before had we led from the front and been in that position to be shot at. That fight to the finish will benefit us in years to come. It was an invaluable experience.

The future will open up for Blackburn Rovers and there is no limit to their ambition. They want more success, more trophies and to conquer Europe. The club will not stand still, and there will be comings and goings, just as there have been in years gone by. Where does Alan Shearer fit into all this? I've lived with speculation about me moving for as long as I can remember. Italy seems to be the most popular destination that others choose for me, but never once have I said that I want to leave Blackburn Rovers.

I am a great believer in fate, and if I am destined to move to Italy one day, then so be it. Until then I'll enjoy my football here in England as much as I always do.

I hope you enjoy yours, too.

HEROES
THE SHEARER DREAM TEAM

I was usually too busy playing on a Saturday to become an avid or regular football watcher, but whenever I had the chance I would watch my beloved Newcastle United playing at St James's Park. I won a competition to spend a day at the training ground once, and the chance to mingle with my heroes made me the happiest lad alive.

If there was a game on television I would be glued to it. You could bet that if there was an outstanding game on the box, me and my mates would be out on the street within minutes of the final whistle, replaying every single incident.

That is when you develop your football idols. Mine came from far and wide, but invariably I would pretend to be the top striker of the day - always wanting to score goals.

If I had to pick my all-time ten favourites, they would be these. They are in no particular order but the man at number one will always be a bit special.

1. KEVIN KEEGAN: He came to Newcastle as a player and transformed the place. I was standing at the Gallowgate End when he made his debut against Queen's Park Rangers, and shouted myself hoarse when he scored with a diving header. It was a moment that will live with me for ever. He breathed new life into the club as a player, just as he has done as a manager. He was only small but very strong, quick and deadly in front of the goal.

I was not alone in worshipping Keegan. When he signed for Newcastle as a player he was like the Pied Piper. Thousands upon thousands of kids flocked to the club to watch him train and play, and drooled over his skills and incredible enthusiasm. I studied and copied loads of players, but Keegan was my number one.

He will live in Newcastle United folk-lore as long as there is a football club.

Here's me with Kevin Keegan. My mum entered my name for a competition our local newspaper ran, for which the prize was a chance to meet him at Newcastle United's training ground. I couldn't believe it when I won, and as you can see from the smile on my face, I was delighted. We've met often since then, but I've never asked him if he remembered this day.

2. PELÉ: He was at his peak long before my time so I never saw him play in a live game, but I have watched him on video and marvelled at his skills. There was not much he couldn't do with a football. He made it appear so easy, it almost looked as if the ball was attached to his body. I remember seeing a clip from the 1970 World Cup finals in Mexico which took my breath away. A ball came in from the wing and Pelé dummied and allowed it to run past the keeper. He collected it from the other side of the area, but shot just wide. It was a moment of genius.

Above: I was too young to watch Pelé play, but I love watching videos of his games for Brazil. He was incredible – such good close skills – and what a goal-scorer!

MARADONA
"Brilliant skills, but his dark side let him down"
Alan Shearer

3. DIEGO MARADONA: Around the time of the 1986 World Cup finals in Mexico the Argentine skipper was the number one player. He was built a bit like Keegan - stocky and muscular - and had marvellous close skills. But he had his darker side which was eventually to prove his downfall. The match against England in Mexico typified the two extremes of his nature. His so-called 'Hand of God' goal, when he punched the ball past Peter Shilton, showed how he was capable of bending the rules to his advantage. But in the same match he ran from the halfway line with the ball at his feet past several defenders to score a goal which few players could equal.

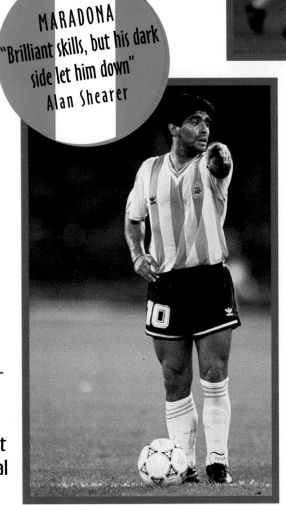

4. KENNY DALGLISH: He is my manager at Blackburn, so I have to choose him in my top ten. But seriously, he was a striker I always admired. When I was twelve, my Uncle David took me to watch Liverpool play Bury in an FA Cup game. It was a great adventure as we travelled by train to Liverpool and

then walked from the station across Stanley Park to Anfield. There I stood on the famous Kop - the envy of all my pals - and marvelled at Dalglish. He was so good at shielding the ball away from his marker with his back to the goal. Chris Nicholl, my manager at Southampton, used to tell me to stick my backside into defenders just like Dalglish and it was a sound piece of advice. He had terrific skills when facing the goal as well, and scored some spectacular goals.

THE SHEARER DREAM TEAM

5. BRYAN ROBSON: He comes from Chester-le-Street in the north-east and I always used to pay particular attention to players from my native area. Robbo was the best English midfield player of his time. He was brave and fearless in the tackle, but I studied him closely for his goal-scoring expertise. He timed his late runs into the box to perfection and would arrive at just the right place to score with a shot or a header.

6. DAVID McCREERY: He first came to notice at Manchester United, but moved to Newcastle. He was only tiny but was a tigerish midfield player and as hard as nails. I remember him well because my Auntie Carol used to look after his kids. When I was just making my mark as a trainee with Southampton, he gave me some useful tips. He would say to me, 'If you can, get your mortgage paid off as quickly as possible.'

Above: Bryan Robson is a real footballing hero of the north-east, especially now that he's back, managing Middlesbrough. He scored an amazing number of goals for a midfield player — only Platty comes close to his record for club and country. These days I get to work with Robbo when there are England get-togethers. He's Terry Venables' number two, and he's a great man to have on the bench for England games. He's very loud; you can't miss his voice. I think he'd still rather be playing though.

McCREERY
"Hard but fair, small but tigerish in the tackle"
Alan Shearer

7. CHRIS WADDLE: Newcastle fans always used to talk about him as the man from the sausage factory in Gateshead who made it to the big time. He was a real working-class hero who made many people's dreams come true. He was tall and lean with a lazy style and he could weave some magic skills on the wing. When he left Newcastle he went on to achieve fame and fortune with Spurs and Marseilles, but I shall always remember him in his black and white striped shirt with a big blue star on the front.

8. PETER SHILTON: I used to enjoy playing in goal for a bit of fun as a lad, and Shilts was always my favourite keeper. He was a fanatical trainer and the supreme professional. I once took five penalties against him when I was a young trainee at Southampton and he saved the lot. Two years later he had moved on to Derby and I came up against him in only my third senior game for The Saints. I caught him with a late challenge and he said to me, 'You won't stay in the game long, young man, if you make tackles like that.'

CHRIS WADDLE
"The sausage maker who made it really big"
Alan Shearer

Right: Peter Shilton in full flight. For a long time he and Ray Clemence shared the England keeper's jersey, swapping it for alternate games almost. He was always my favourite, especially as a lad when I played between the sticks. He was the Saints keeper when I joined them, and I enjoyed trying to put the ball past him. I succeeded sometimes!

TEN TOP TIPS
ON GOING FOR GOAL

1. Always keep your eye on the ball. It is a simple piece of advice but as with any ball game such as tennis, golf, rugby etc., if you do not keep your head still and focus on the ball you will never make a good enough contact with it to place it where you want to.

2. Always hit the target. You have to develop a good positional sense and try to keep a picture in your mind of where the goal is situated. Then, when the ball comes your way, you have to launch your attempt at goal as quickly as possible. You will never score if your shooting or heading misses the target.

3. Be hungry for goals. Never be satisfied with your tally. Always go looking for one more. It pays to be selfish at times, but do not overdo this. If a team-mate is in a much better goal-scoring position than you, it will benefit your team to pass the ball to him. Then when the roles are reversed, there is a good chance he will return the favour.

4. Always follow up shots at goal. If a colleague is having a shot, do not just stand back and watch. Sprint towards the goal and if the goalkeeper fails to hold the ball, there is sometimes a simple tap-in goal to be had. They might not be spectacular, but they all count.

5. Develop heading skills. Timing is very important, so practise jumping and climbing to head the ball. It is crucial to keep your eyes on the ball and make contact with your forehead. As you get older and stronger, you can use your neck muscles to generate extra power. So many goals are scored from corners and free kicks these days that good heading ability is essential.

6. Become a penalty expert. There are some rich pickings to be had from the spot but it's not as easy as it looks. Make your mind up where you are going to place the ball - and never change it. I have paid the price for doing that in the past, and the keeper has saved my shot.

7. Work on your pace and sharpness. Today's game is so quick and competitive, often a split second can make all the difference in turning a half-chance into a goal. Short, sharp sprints are ideal practice sessions. Forget about marathon runs. It pays to think and react quickly in a crowded penalty area.

8. Develop a sound and unflappable temperament. Often you will find yourself up against two or three defenders who will be trying to kick you to stop you scoring. It is sometimes hard not to retaliate but you have to grin and bear it. Walk away. The best way to get back at them is to score a goal - better still, make it a hat-trick.

9. Be brave. There is so much physical contact in football that you have to be prepared for plenty of knocks. The striker who is willing to throw himself in among the flying boots is usually the one who scores most goals. The odd bruise is worth it to add one to your total.

10. Be accurate. Often you only see a gap for a fraction of a second and you have to rifle the ball through it into the net. If you are not accurate enough with your shot, the chance will go begging. I take some time out after each training session to have some shots at goal. Even if there is no goalkeeper around, I will try to place the ball firmly and accurately into a chosen area of the net.

ALAN SHEARER

DATE OF BIRTH
13 August 1970 (zodiac sign - Leo the Lion!)

SCHOOLS FOOTBALL
School: Gosforth High
Area: Newcastle (represented at all levels, from age 11 onwards)
Northumberland County: Represented Under 15s - seasons 1983/84 & 1984/85; represented Under 19s - season 1985/86

JUNIOR FOOTBALL
Wallsend Boys Club: Age groups up to and including season 1985/86
Cramlington Juniors: Season 1985/86
* Cramlington Juniors won the NFA (county) cup, an Under 18 competition, with an Under 16 side. The winning goal came from a penalty taken by Alan Shearer in the last minute (the penalty was awarded for a foul on Alan himself!)

SOUTHAMPTON FC
Signed Associated Schoolboy: 7 September 1984
Final pre-YTS assessment: Easter 1986 at Gurney Dixon Centre, Lymington
Signed YTS trainee: 4 July 1986
First season as trainee: Season 1986/87
* Club top scorer with 31 goals while trainee
First team debut as sub: 26 March 1988 at Stamford Bridge. Beat Chelsea 1-0
First team debut (full): 1988 at The Dell. Beat Arsenal 4-2. Alan scored a hat-trick, while still a YTS trainee
* Youngest player to score a hat-trick in the First Division
* Youngest player to score a hat-trick on his debut
First pro contract signed: 12 April 1988

BLACKBURN ROVERS FC
Transferred: 27 July 1992 - then record fee in the UK
League debut: 15 August 1992. Crystal Palace (3) v Blackburn (3). Scored 2

ENGLAND
Under 17s debut: 16 February 1988 at Stoke. Beat Republic of Ireland 2-1. Scored 1
Under 18s debut: May 1988. Close of season tournament in Switzerland
Under 21s debut as sub: 16 October 1990 v Poland at Tottenham. Lost 1-0: on for last 12 minutes
Under 21s debut (full): 13 November 1990. Beat Republic of Ireland 3-0: scored 2
First hat-trick: 29 May 1991 v Mexico at Toloun. Won 6-0
First captain: 31 May 1991 v USSR at Toloun. Won 2-1. Scored 1
* Record U21 goals: 13 goals in 11 full games
Full international debut: 19 February 1992 v France at Wembley. Won 2-0. Scored 1
To date (end of 1994/95 season): 17 caps, 5 goals

**SEASON'S TOP SCORER WITH 37 GOALS
WINNER OF THE GOLDEN BOOT AWARD
PFA PLAYER OF THE YEAR 1994/95**

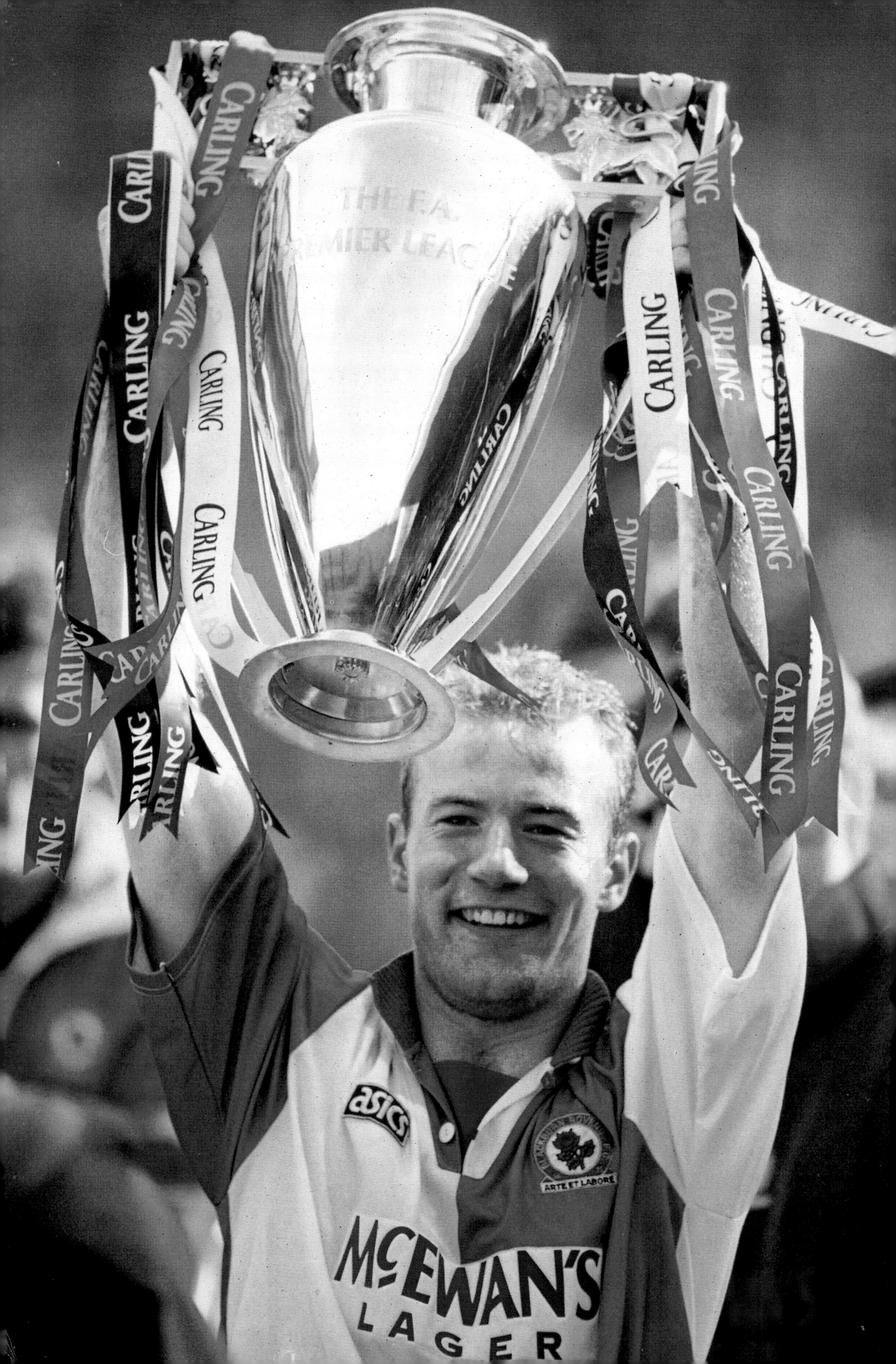
THE F.A.
PREMIER LEAG
CARLING
ARTE ET LABORE
McEWAN'S
LAGER